This book is dedicated to my Inner Child,
Inner Teen and Highest Self for getting me
through the days where hope was hard to find.

Words I Wish I Heard That I Gift To You

M. MUSE

Words I Wish I Heard That I Gift To You. Is a true act of love; it is filled with the words that I often need to hear when I am going through difficult periods in my life. I know that so many of us battle things in private and need to hear somebody tell us that everything is going to be okay, even if it isn't right now. Sometimes we just need a hand and for someone to let us know that through these murky waters of our mind, they see us clearly and they know that we are a good person. They know that we will be okay. They know that we are worthy of good things. They know that we can get through this and stand in the light of our best selves. We don't always have someone to physically sit with us and tell us these things, so I wrote this book to say them to you. So that you know that wherever you are and whatever you are going through, someone is in your corner, and they understand.

- M.Muse x

*May I find it within to give myself the kindness
that I have given others.*

- M.Muse

If the moon be a taker of day, for you, my love, I will shun it away because nighttime does raise the wrath of anxiety in your heart. I will battle the knights of the dark and force them to place dresser in place when your mind sees a face. I will command the tap to stop leaking, which you confuse with floorboards squeaking and intruders encroaching. I will protect you from your own imagination. I will cover you, lathering you in the affection of my love, and reign prosperity through you. I will watch you flourish without fear of what your mind may tell you. With me, you are safe during the night and the day.

It's okay to cry, to have your tears ask the whys that your mind cannot yet describe, it just knows that it is in a state that it shouldn't be in, and wants nothing more than to drain itself of the torment of this plague, it is okay to cry, to let all that is rotting inside, leak and release you of the illness that curdles your stomach and causes your teeth to grit, as its pain shoots through your nerves and leaves you weak, it is okay to cry, to cry so hard that your mouth cannot describe the exact reason why, to pant, and yelp and howl, to roar into your pillow until it is flooded and gasping for air, for you are allowing these emotions to free in their reckless tides, it is okay to cry, to want to pour out all that is troubling you inside and see it scattered out in front of you, so that you may find peace or next action, because things are always a little easier when they are no longer being forced to hide. My love, cry.

The joy you seek is closer than you think. It is in the moments when you allow yourself to shine without fearing that your light will blind those around you, you deserve to allow yourself to be and relish in the tranquillity of your authenticity.

I know nothing of a world that is better without you being in it. It does not exist; the only space in which it lives is within your mind, but you will find that in this lifetime, in this world that we share, we need you here. We need your laugh, we need your smile, we need your heart that is filled with a gracious goodness that blesses us all, we need your energy, we need you here. I know sometimes life has a way of making hours feel like days, and your mind can be a horrible place, filled with landmines buried in pasts less explored, festered with wicked words that you would have never known had people not engraved them upon your throne. I am sorry that you find yourself too comfortable with their lies. I want you to hear me when I say, we need you in this world today and in the wonder of all of the adventures that will follow the next day, because I promise you will be okay. I just need you to stay here with us, okay? Please stay.

Please just know that it's okay that you're not okay right now. If you can't take my calls or answer my texts, if you need time for yourself right now and don't have the energy to engage with me as we once did, I won't take it personally. My love for you won't change. I will be here with a notepad full of the moments that you aren't around for, and I will keep my thoughts fresh so you can get my immediate feelings. I will take photos of the sunsets that you are missing in your dark room as your mind robs you of the lightness that you once loved. I will create tabs for all of the places I only want to visit if I am with you, because our time together is my favorite. I will research how best to be a friend to you as you heal. You have a safe space with me to share how you feel. I will be waiting patiently to see your name flash onto my screen, and my heart will leap at the chance to have you back with me. I promise not to be too loud because I know silence has a way of being the loudest when it is not welcomed. Your ears must be sensitive, so I will whisper and be as soft and gentle as you need. I will wait for you to say 'Hi' first, and then I will say it all to you and annoy you, cry with you, laugh with you, smile with you, and welcome you back home. You can tell me everything or nothing at all. I know there is a period of adjustment after weathering the turmoil of mental storms. Just know I am here, and there is no moving on if you aren't by my side. There's no rush; *please take your time.*

Lather yourself in the comfort of knowing that new days will come, new feelings will run a parade, and new ways of seeing the world will relieve your tired eyes of their night shift, for you have been cramped by the darkness for too long. Newness will bring life, and maybe take away the ache of the old, but I think that is exactly what you need. A chance to unwind and explore the endless breadth of life, to sit with self and see the beauty that comes alive when you are no longer simply trying to survive.

Isn't it better to feel alive than feel nothing at all, to freefall into the fields of realities that sing for your picking, for you to just make a choice and crash into its welcoming, to see, explore, and find all of the parts of yourself that are birthed in the fruitful turmoil of the unknown, but trusting with everything in your gut that whatever comes from this will be worth it? Isn't it better to just live and not be in a constant state of worry? The future has its plans laid out, and there is nothing that we can do until we get there, so why fret on the months that have not come or the ones that have passed while ignoring the passion of our present? Isn't it better to have the stories, to be able to say that you did it, even when you thought you couldn't, even when life gave you ample reason to hermit and live within yourself, but you did it? You stepped out and into the field; you picked the petals of millions of realities and explored them, allowing your soul to venture into the realms of thousands of versions of you. Isn't it better to live than to watch your life pass you by. Isn't it better to have lived and tried?

All of us are fighting for it, to experience our own little pockets of bliss, just remember if you don't have it yet, someone else's story started like this. Your moment is coming soon.

There will be moments that feel like silent confirmations between you and the universe—a pat on the head, a gentle nudge on the soft of your back, a whispered wink, a go ahead, a promise that your steps forward are protected, and you, in all of your glory and all of your divinity are going to be perfectly alright as you step into the next season of your life.

The thing about goodbyes is that they shouldn't be difficult to bring to the surface because they are mothered in deep thought and confirmed with the painful sensation of a decision made, a sharp ache in the mind as it replays all of the good times, but the hearts burning lets you know that it is time to say the very thing you had been trying to tame, as you tried to reframe the bad times and make them droplets amongst the vastness of the pond, but thoughts of them seem to intrude on silent nights, where adorning memories once lied and set you softly into the stream of the night, you find memories of them televised with the volume set to high, no sleep may be found. You do weep with tired tears, because years have been invested, and goodbyes seem to summon fears and doubts. They make even the most secure feel insecure because there is something so promising about its finality. Very few work their way back from its landing, but it must be done because the heart is furious with your constant breaking and repairing; it is wearing out, trying to find depth in loose breaths; it cannot deal with the limbo anymore. So goodbye is the only open door for you to explore.

Hey there, pumpkin, my wonder child with the free spirit mothering a heavy heart, you are a figment of beauty's imagination, birthed with the soul of Aphrodite. You seem to leave little trails of your love behind you, your name floating in conversations, and descriptions of your warmth seem to swarm the minds of those that met you once. You are an anomaly in a world that cannot deal with the preciousness of a pearl that yearns for gentle encounters but refuses to shatter in the face of life's less graceful nature.

Aren't you lovely? Lovely in spirit, lovely in heart, lovely in the way that you seek to start your day with words of love and reasons to smile, enjoying the present without fretting about the future's woes, you are lovely in all senses of the word, so beautifully lovely, yes, you.

There will never be another you; how wonderful is that? To know that all that you are is perfectly yours, nobody can emulate it; nobody can retrace your steps and see, experience, or feel the way that you do because it was all meant for you. You have been given this treasure of life, and I watch you grapple with it, trying to push it away from yourself, but life and living are meant for you, I promise. All that you have been through was to prepare you for a future so bright that it makes day and night one entity because it glows with such conviction. You are destined for abundance, peace, and ease; it is all coming to you. I know you seem to wish that you weren't yourself sometimes, but you are one of a kind. You know darkness so well that you can recognize light in all of its forms. That is why you can see the souls that hold the pureness of life's light because you have seen the tormenting nature on the other side. You are divine in all that you are, *please stop wishing to be anyone but yourself upon shooting stars.*

My love, I have every belief that you will create a beautiful life for yourself, one that squeezes you soo tight at the end of the night and dances through the air even when you feel heavy in the mundane nature of life. I trust that your future will see you laugh more than you cry, that you will never have a dry eye when you are surrounded by the friends that will come into your life because laughter and emotional vulnerability will be a part of the loving medicine you receive from them. I trust that you will eat foods that comfortably satisfy you, you'll sit in chairs without placing pillows on your lap, you'll look at yourself in reflections and smile at the person who smiles back, you will rest without worry, you will shine without fear, and you will sit down at the end of the year with eyes that shine as fireworks alight in the distance of a house that feels like home for the first time. And you will smile toothy and large because you know more beautiful days are coming your way. *For a beautiful life was always a part of your fate*

Make space within yourself for the unplanned, allow beautiful mistakes to happen, watch yourself ride the wave of the new direction for this section of your life, do not fight the places that beautiful mistakes will introduce you to because I promise you these places were called to you by the divine, allow yourself to enjoy the time of disrupted routines, walks that lead you to streams of thought forested with creation and reflection, swim along the tides that introduce you to a softer life, fall in love with exploring who you are outside of your plans, enjoy the way that the universe holds your hand and encourages you to listen to your gut, step gut first into the unknown beauty of life's beautiful mistakes. Never planned, but always destined to help you step with grace into the future that awaits.

Oh, my love, I wish you knew how untrue the words that you speak to yourself are. Those heart-breaking thoughts that you allow to pass your lips and sit comfortably in your mind for your inner child to find. Such cruel thoughts should not have freedom with you; they are not true. You are a kind soul, with a mind that deserves to be consoled. You are beautiful. You are kind. You are worthy of people's time. You are deserving of the love that is coming your way. You are aligned with the blessings found every day. You are so special to me. I know that you've recited horrible thoughts to yourself and created a mantra of self-hatred, but you have never deserved it. Not when the first person said it to you, and not now that you believe it to be true. You deserve kinder thoughts. You are the best thing that you could ever be. *I happen to think that you are fucking incredible.*

We ask the universe to show us how amazing we are and we cry when things change, when people and circumstances are taken away because we were comfortable in the disaster that we had confused for home, we don't realize that in our requests there is an exchange, to be given is to be taken away, we cannot stay in the dirt and then welcome in new life, it will never survive beneath the toxic environment that we learnt to survive within, we don't realize that sometimes in order to win, is to see that we have grown beyond the mess we were stuck in, sometimes we have to see that there are people perfectly designed to be all that you need, their souls align with you and seek to see you chuckle in euphoric peace, they are not pleased or at ease in your self-sacrifice to keep their egos alight. If you ask the universe to show you how amazing you are, be prepared to let go of the things that have burdened you from the start. To be given, is to be taken away.

Oh, my love, I wish you realised just how well you are doing. This is all so new. Sometimes you will lose patience with yourself, as do I. You may fall into a room of thoughts that have locked the doors and won't let you leave for a day or a week, as have I. You may find yourself feeling disconnected from people and all that surrounds you, as do I. You may realise that you want to quit your job and start a new career. I'm right there with you. You may realise that you are in need of all the energy that you once used to please people around you, as have I. You may find yourself looking back at events in your life with a new set of eyes and finding yourself forced to heal wounds that you didn't know had such deep roots, as have all who are healing. Healing is messy; it's picking up the pieces of yourself and learning to love the beauty and the ugly all the same. It can fill you up, but it will deflate you before it blesses you with the soundness of knowing yourself. You are doing amazingly. You are doing it your way, and with time, you will realise that there was never a right way to do it; you just had to go through it. Trust me, my angel, you are doing it beautifully and as you are being called to.

I have to ask you, my love, what is the end goal here? I know you have your fears; you feel like if you stop yourself from doing it, you're in the clear, your desires will subside, and you can get on with life. You've sabotaged yourself so many times. Why not just allow yourself to try? I know there is a lot of vulnerability in trying to make it happen, but the further you run, the more you feel you've failed. Why not just face yourself and see what you can do before shrinking away due to the things that people project onto you? They have no idea how much magic resides within you, because if they knew, I promise they would push you to trust in all that your soul calls you to do.

Precious are the people who have felt pain and do everything in their power not to make others feel the same. How grossly beautiful it is to know agony in such an intimate way that you know that it isn't worth imprinting its wrath onto someone else. I pray that healing finds the depths of your sorest wounds and blooms blessed flowers that take all pain from you. I pray your days hold the lightness that hums graciously within you, and I pray your future provides justice for the things you've been through. *I pray the purest form of love follows and surrounds you.*

We so often say, damned if I do, damned if I don't. What if it was blessed if I do, blessed if I don't? Because blessings will follow me effortlessly as I explore the destiny that calls to me, and every choice will always bring me something worthy of praise. So, there is no right or wrong; there is no need to hold on and control because I know I am blessed if I do, blessed if I don't, blessed if I will, and blessed if I won't. Blessed to experience all that is aligned with me.

Give yourself grace; you are trying your best. I see it. You are putting in the time; you are doing all of the scary but necessary things. You are showing up for yourself in a way that you never have before. I know that there is a part of you that is worried that it will all be for nothing, but I need you to silence that voice. You have no idea of the kind of blessings that are awaiting you. Lock in, give up your need for control, and keep trying. *I promise it will all be worth it.*

Why not you? You have become comfortable with affirming deceitful untruths because they comfort you. You think it is better to stay in a space that comforts and suffocates you than to give into the flow of life that you feel pulling you. You have framed your decisions around the idea that it could never be you. But, why not you? I see no reason why you shouldn't find yourself dancing amongst life's most wonderful affairs, bearing fruit of delight and fulfilment; you are deserving of it all. I know that there is a calling in the shadows of your past that tries to tame your hope, but I dare you to hope regardless of its sinister serenade. You were made with Cupid's love, and you shine even in your stillness, for you are a blessing on Earth. So, please hear me when I say, yes, you. Yes, you, who smiles with all of your teeth and then gets shy. Yes, you who dreams of a life that smothers you with adventure. Yes, you who seeks peace. Yes, you, who is learning what it means to love yourself. Yes, you, who was an adult before your time. Yes, you, who is learning how to trust the divine. Yes, you, who everyone told that it couldn't be. I need you to trust me when I say that it is you who deserves to see the beauty of blessed days. Yes, You. *Always, You.*

Oh my love, sometimes the best that we can do is not wish our
lives away

Happiness looks good on you; it fills the starless sky with twinkles of light. I ask that you please, wear your joy and place harmony in the mourning that the world is in. To see somebody happy will remind the rest of us that we can get there too. One day, we can dance in the bliss of life with you.

Sometimes a goodbye can be a see you soon or a gratitude-filled farewell for the memories that will keep you both awake at night as you smile looking at your ceiling, while your heart mourns the moments together but smiles at the fact that you got to have them. *You were happy. You were loved.*

There are these wonderful souls that are placed amongst us, those that feel everything with their entire being , feelings run through them freely and they welcome them all because they have learnt that to block them is to harden themselves, for their softness is found in their hearts desire to understand the heart of another, these people are soul filled lovers, it is not the person they see but the soul that shines back at them as they watch you, they have this ability to just understand people, like a divine line that tells them of the times when you were alone with no-one to hold you, they see right through, they see all of you and accept every single tiny piece of you, because they desire that acceptance to. They are birthed with the gift of feeling, and I find that they have felt the harshest of souls who have fed from their light, and they have screamed as tears ripped through them in the dead of the night, yet they still fight because they know that there is light to be found in this world of darkness. To the wonderful souls with the ability to feel, I pray your soul finds those who give you space to bask in their warmth and heal, I pray people make space for you to also share how you feel, I pray you are surrounded by love that is shown and not simply said, I pray you allow yourself rest and invest some of the beauty that glows within you into yourself, I pray the gentle love that you place into this world bathes you in all that you do. I pray that you never stop being you.

You cannot apologise for who you are becoming in this season of your life. I know you feel that burning in the pit of your stomach as you notice the little synchronicities that follow you daily; they are letting you know that the future is padded with all that your heart calls for and more. I know that there is a part of you that is sure that this is the period of your life that you have been fighting for, please do not block your blessings by letting people lessen the glow that throws itself around you and illuminates all that you do. There is a glow that is shielding you from the patterns that once comforted you. The sun does not apologise for the way it illuminates our homes in the summertime, for it is its season of abundant glow and the natural flow of birth and death. Do not apologise for how you shine in this season of your life; glow unapologetically and welcome the birthing of new life.

You ask me, what if I get it all wrong? And I say, "What a blessing to have tried and got it all wrong and now know what you need to do to get it right. We are all scared of getting it wrong, but we don't realise the power it takes to get it wrong, the courage it takes to do it even when you have no idea what you are doing, or the lessons you learn by understanding everything that you would never do again. We seem to forget that in order to understand these things, we have to get them wrong. What a special thing to be able to define what you don't want for yourself, to be able to welcome in all that is right for you. I'm not saying that it's easy, but I know that there is something to be celebrated in doing your best and learning from all of the outcomes. Getting it wrong isn't the scariest thing that can happen to you; never trying is."

I am so proud of you. I know this whole transition isn't easy, and at times it feels lonely, like nobody understands why it is so necessary for you to let go of the person that they once knew in order to step into the most authentic version of you. I do. I know that being who they needed you to be was exhausting. You struggled to understand the difference between what you wanted from life and what you were told you wanted from life. You attained the things that made those around you proud, but you still struggled to feel found. You found yourself lost, thrashing in waves of undiscovered possibilities that were calling your name and begging you to take a chance on yourself. To let go of the comfortable and conforming and step into the growing and exploring. I want you to know it is all going to be worth it, and they will eventually understand when they see how you thrive by taking charge of your own life, how resilient and full of life you become when you are your own number one, how your smile blesses without weighted hesitation because although life isn't perfect, it is being lived for you, so every lesson and blessing feels worth it. I am so proud of you.

I hope beautiful experiences follow you into spaces that resurface feelings rooted in places that didn't give you such grace. I know at times the world feels like a scary place for you. I hope beautiful moments surround you and bathe you in the warmth of their light.

I hope you have the courage to live a life that brings you joy. So many of us are worn out by the time we reach our mid-twenties, and the prospect of life beyond that feels bleak and unremarkable. We entered with all of these ideas of what life would look like for us, and as we settle into the humdrum, our radiance becomes like sprinklers. Momentary brightness in peak inspiration, only to dwindle into spits of light. You deserve so much more. I hope you have the courage to go for the life that you see in your dreams—the vividly coloured landscape of possibility that crashes through your mind in its beautiful silence. I know such a thing comes with sacrifice, but what could be more worthy of sacrifice than living a life that feels aligned? To slowly implement the practices, mental foundations, and boundaries needed to thrive in a way that makes life feel worth it again. I hope we find the courage to make it happen, because I know that there are versions of us who have already done it and they await our arrival. They keep showing us what it could be because we are more than capable of making it happen. Oh, my love, I hope we have the courage to try and not sit on the sidelines for the rest of our lives.

There may be days when breathing is painful. To simply inhale may feel like a task; you may find yourself fighting to even start your day, to keep your flow without returning to bed. I just want you to know that's okay. It is okay that you are not okay right now. Life is fucking difficult, but the fact that you woke up and tried your best... my love, I can ask no more of you. I am so proud of you for showing up for yourself in any way that you were able to. You have no idea how much brighter the world shines by having you in it.

Thank you for being here

I hope you find the strength to leave the people, situations, and spaces that no longer fit who you have become. You have blossomed into a being of life's greatest potential because you took the time to destroy your own infected weeds, you tended to your garden on bended knees, and you took the time to plant it tranquilly. You tended to it daily, singing to it if it needed it, providing it with emotional support as it weathered the wars of nature's seasonal swings. You cut out the flowers that tried to bloom a poisonous beauty that looked familiar but no longer connected with you emotionally because you now know that you deserve better. You have tended to your garden with such a sympathetic hand, completely understanding that it would take time for so much light to derive from such wounded soils. And yet, here you stand. Beautifully bloomed with a mind that understands that you are special. Yet, I see you still holding on to what once was beyond the outskirts of such a wonderful creation. I see the petals wither a little as you come in from work; I see the leaves curl into themselves as you get ready to see your "friends." I see the roots slowly ingesting infection as you swallow your boundaries and let your family trample all over your dreams. It seems that you are only comfortable blooming on your own. I just hope you find the strength to realise that you can roam this Earth with your garden adorning you and watch the life you have created manifest in all that you do, but the sacrifice is that you might have to let go of the people, situations, and spaces that you once knew.

One day, all that we are worrying about right now will no longer exist. We will look back at these moments as our new worries call for our attention and think about how silly we were to worry because it all worked out in the end. Maybe not as we wanted it to, but as it had to. It makes me wonder if any worry is ever worth being so worrisome about, because they all have their time, don't they? Worries. They arrive, fill up our rooms, and keep us awake at night until we do our best to sort them, and then we find that they go. Until another places its heavy palms on our shoulders, and we find ourselves weighted by its arrival. I like to think that one day we will learn not to worry because we will have come to the realisation that life plays by its own rules and that, in the end, everything passes in its own time. All worries eventually wash away. We just have to take it day by day.

There is so much joy to be had in a life that you make worth living, one that you fill with joyous moments of ease and open sensitivity without fearing the beauty of the power-filled exchange, we are deserving and I know that thought may feel unnerving, but I beg of you, dear one, to drain yourself of the ideas that have birthed in the incubator of trauma. Fly amongst the fluttered vibrations of the butterfly's that beg to guide you home and into the palms of a life that Pinky promises you rosy cheeks and tearful eyes that don't dry, for they are always glistening with the excitement of new minute and the wonder that it seeks to offer. Dear child, there is so much that life wants to offer you, I just ask that you allow yourself to take hold of its hand.

When something within us dies, does it make space for the flowering of a new source of life? I mean, that's what we're taught, right? With death comes life, and nothing in this world is simply bad because a blessing will be birthed from its tragedy. Demolished trees create a raging breeze that gives fallen leaves the push they need to find new ground. If this concept of life is true, I choose to find peace in its sentiment. When a part of us dies, we are making space for something beautiful to happen within our lives; a figment of beauty is destined to be birthed from such pain. I will find comfort in the parts of me that die again and again.

I know it is not easy to be so beautifully vulnerable amidst the madness of the world, you are constantly open to the newness of pain birthed in nations far from yours but your heart aches for the lives destroyed by a world that cannot agree that we are all worthy of peace, I see the way that your body curls into itself until you are nothing more than a speck amongst the rubbles of emotions that have peaked in your room, you resume placement on bed and rest your head lazily on your pillow and a willow blooms from your tears, and surrounds you protectively, too gentle for the chaos of this world, so soft, so gentle, so beautiful, your soul.

I wish you peace. I wish you the kind of peace that simmers from the core of your being and spreads its warmth through you in moments when it seems scarce. I wish you the kind of peace that never allows you to feel lonely, but accepting of your own presence when you are alone, for you are able to be the observer of your thoughts without drowning in their reckless waves. I wish you peace in the relationships that you surround yourself with. May the people blessed with access to your light know how to treat you right and may consideration for you never be an afterthought, but a forthcoming blessing bestowed upon you. I wish you peace from the places where your peace was robbed. If I had the power to revisit the scenes of your past that feel all too present and bundle your lost joy and place it back into you, I would, so that you may know what peace you could have without the loss of pieces of you. I wish you a peace so entirely consuming that it makes your present moments something to savor because I know that life hasn't always been easy. *I wish you peace.*

The scary yet comforting thing about life is that it just keeps moving. Even in our stillness, we are changing, so if you feel like you aren't moving forward; let me remind you that you are. No second is the same; the thoughts change; your leg twitches, your finger scrolls, your tummy rolls with anxiety or excitement, and your blood circulates with a steady current. You are moving forward and changing, even if you don't feel like it. Life is easing us in the direction we so deeply fear but need. *Forward.*

I am watching you fall in love with the way today tastes. I see it in the luminosity of your orbs that jump with excitement as the sun places summer berries on the tip of your nose as you wake up. I see it in the way you hopscotch to the bathroom and groove to the world's tunes as you brush your teeth. I see it in the clothes that you once neglected for their brightness made you feel too seen, being selected joyously as you and the warm hues that decorate our room high-five at the selection of your orange dungarees. I see it in the way you run to your canvas and paint, and your hair falls lazily around your shoulders, unable to keep up with this new taste for life, and you grant it peace by packing it lovingly into a bun at the top of your head, held together by paint brushes that have seen better days but will see a better day, for today is the day that life has reintroduced you to yourself. I see you falling in love with the way each day tastes, some more sour than the last, but I watch you bask in the flavour profile and season your day with ways to fit your flavouring. I am watching you realise that life loves you, and you are beginning to love it too.

Place one foot in front of the other, do not fret of step last placed for it has passed and you are fast moving to a future that is decorated with the softness you always deserved, there is a part of your soul that has always called you forward, even when forward felt cruel and uninviting, it whispered and with time learnt to roar for it knew with absolute power and absolute cheer that you were destined to move beyond the heaviness that saw you fight to be here. So, I ask that you stride with your head held high and your soul feeling alive, because you my love, were always meant to thrive. So please, just Take, It, One, Step, At, A, Time.

Your feelings are valid; stop invalidating them to force yourself to keep the peace with someone who destroys yours.

Just as you are, you are enough. It never fails to amaze me how beautiful it is that you are so willing to grow and let life flow through you while learning to accept yourself. I know that it is easy to get wrapped up in all of the ways that you need to take away from yourself, but I think there is beauty to be found in the way that you accept and love the person that you are right now. Someone so open to change, open to healing, learning to accept that feeling doesn't make you weak. You are enough today and all of the days of this week. You don't need to add or take away to be enough, who you are in this moment is the perfect amount of everything, my love.

I hope you allow yourself to lean into this desire that you have to create. I hope you let your mind run wild with ideas that can only reach their full potential if you birth them into this world. I hope you stop giving into the voice of your doubts and remind yourself that if you have the idea, it is because there is kindling within your soul that knows that you are more than capable of making it happen. I hope that you remind yourself that even if it takes a while, simply showing up makes you an incredible artist. Whether that is once a week, once a month, or once a year, to show up and put your best foot forward to make your ideas come to fruition takes great courage. So, I ask that you lean shamelessly into your desire to create. I know that your mind is calling you to step into the greatness of your artistic fate.

Do you want to know what I am looking forward to? The day it all makes sense to you, the day you realise that all that you have gone through was to bring you this overwhelmingly full moment that sets your soul on fire, because you see it, you see yourself crying in your room, you see yourself isolating, you see yourself fighting for life, you see yourself learning to like yourself before you loved yourself, and you realise right in that moment that it was to bring you here. My love, I know it feels so far away, and I am in it with you. I just know that whatever is coming is the blessing that follows for all that you have been through.

You can't outrun what is meant for you. I know you want to. I know you want to shrink yourself and hide from everybody because your past has shown you that when you are seen, people are mean. But baby, there are spaces waiting for you, and the truth is, they will still be there in 13 years if you decide to run for that long, that dissatisfaction that dissatisfaction that is eating you up at night is because you know that you aren't living in your light. You have been given a gift that only you can share. There are people waiting for you to be their new favourite; there are discoveries that are waiting for you to unravel them; there are people waiting to hear your words and connect with you; there is someone manifesting your talents to arrive and shift their whole life; and there are companies waiting to hear all of your wonderful ideas. Most importantly, there is a child within you that wants you to live beyond your fears. Don't stall your greatness; we aren't promised our years.

What if the joy that seeks to follow you after this pain is no match for the joy you had before? Oh, my love, I know that's a scary thought. But I ask you this: what if the joy that you find after this is just different, neither better nor worse, but more fitting for the person that you become once you've gotten through this? What if the next joy is the best joy for the new you?

My heart aches to know that we make a home in the darkness. We get used to sitting in it, used to the feeling of the lows. At times, we prefer it. We spend our highs navigating anxiety first as we await the dreaded drop to reality that has become all too familiar to us. We start to believe that happiness doesn't come without self-sacrifice or a payoff that is too expensive for us to afford, for we are running on empty emotionally. So, we spend our highs waiting to once again return to the darkness. Only once we get there do we realise how grateful and present we should have been to have had a moment that allowed us to just be and be happy.

Goodbyes hurt, sometimes the goodness in them is hard to find because of the pain that is left behind.

Sometimes we are the cause of our own pain. We feel sick from the wounds that others have inflicted on us, and we eventually get stuck. It becomes difficult for us to even live, so we don't. Instead, we get used to existing: sleep, work, eat, phone time, and repeat. Dying in mindless routine and finding some kind of hope in the happiness of others, all while slowly fraying beneath the pain of knowing that we could. We could if we tried. We could be that person; we could do those things; that could be us, but we spend so much time in the wonderland of could that we never do. We get stuck in a cycle of pain, allowing ourselves to believe that happiness doesn't know our name because to remain in pain seems better than to try for happiness and fail. We cause our own pain by stopping ourselves from having the opportunity to live again.

Stop getting over it. It's time to get through it.

Your struggles with your mental health do not make you unlovable. It does not mean that you are unworthy of a butterfly filled stomach, someone to stroke your one lonesome tear that gracefully grazes your cheeks after a joke has left you feeling deliciously weak, the subtle warmth of a peck of reassurance, the frenzied panic that fuels your body to call your friend after getting the first 'wanna go on a date?' text, the awkwardness of that first date that slowly disappears as you realise the beauty found in both of you choosing to be there, someone to run through the rain with as you both laugh whilst your clothes cling to you and you squeeze through the busyness of the night, someone to engulf you with their essence as they hold you on your darkest days and give you space when you need it most. You deserve to be loved, to feel the cuddled comfort of life's rawest emotions, and to feel safe in someone's devotion. My love, you are worthy of love.

Life's uncertainty can't stop you from making decisions that you know with guttural certainty you want to make. Tomorrow will always come, until one day it doesn't. And I hate the thought of you missing out on your own life because you were so worried about *getting it right.*

Sometimes you just have to hold onto the hope that it will get better. Move with the expectation that life is going to offer you abundant reasons to be hopeful and allow that feeling to fuel and consume you. That feeling when your breath catches in your throat as you see the light at the end of the tunnel, that moment of ease after chasing sanity for months on end, the deep gulp of air that gently cools your lungs as you get to where you have been manifesting, it is that moment. That tiny window of something other than the turmoil that you live in every day, that is what you need to hold onto. Sometimes hope is all we have to cherish on heavy days.

We are all growing constantly. Sometimes the growth doesn't feel painful; in fact, it feels easy. You feel no sense of resistance because, deep inside, you know it's right. Other times, it is strenuous. It pushes you beyond your breaking point and forces you to realise that maybe, just maybe, you are a hell of a lot stronger than you give yourself credit for.

There is no worse feeling than when somebody stops feeling like home; it's a slow eviction notice with you both frantically trying to fix unbroken experiences and making the fault yours. Forgetting that in life we are ever changing, and our relationship will face the pain of rearranging, we must not fight the separation if it feels right. Sometimes home isn't home forever; it is a space dedicated for otherworldly joy to be captured within, a space to revisit mentally but not physically. *It is time for you both to move on with memories of the home you built together.*

Some days, you just won't feel like yourself. Your favourite song will no longer feel like your favourite. Your morning coffee will taste too sour, even when made exactly as you like it. You will feel a lot more tired while doing less. Your body won't settle comfortably as you try to rest. Your food won't seem as appealing as it did the day before when you were craving it. When you look in the mirror, you may find yourself feeling disconnected from the person who looks back at you. Some days are just sad days. Where the overwhelming heaviness of tears settles behind our eyes and waits for any reason to let go and cry. One time, it was the opening scene of Mama Mia for me. And that's okay. My love, it's okay to have a bad day or as many bad days as you need, but please remember that the person that you are right now is a beautiful representation of your resilience, your kindness, and your love. Please be gentle with yourself on those bad days. *Being mean to yourself doesn't make them go away.*

My love, you must be exhausted.

It can't be easy being strong all the time. I wish that I could wrap my arms around you and let you lean entirely into me while I take the weight off your shoulders. I wish that I could give you the comfort that you seek. I wish that I could be the person to show you that your feelings don't make you weak. I wish I could sit in silence with you, speak with you, sing with you, and dream with you. Show you that there is safety in people, and you don't have to be on guard. You deserve to feel safe with someone beyond yourself. I would love for you to one day realise that you don't always have to be strong; life is a little easier when you have someone to lean on.

Accepting help doesn't make you weak. In a world full of difficulty, blessed are the people who seek to share the responsibility of the minds of those who have suffered through things they struggle to share. It is hard to be there, in a place where you know you cannot do it alone this time, because the things that you have always feared to find, have had a new wind of life and are playing out the details in your mind's eye all at once. Piling onto the pillar of mental health that was struggling to hold itself together, for it has weathered tornadoes far too rough for one mind to deal with. I know you have become accustomed to not sharing the weight of the thoughts that trudge through your mind, but you may find now is the right time to allow someone to help you figure it all out. It's not easy; it's scary to share the nightmares that you have hidden from yourself, but that may be why it is time to welcome in the comfort of having somebody else to see you through this. I know you can do it again; you have picked yourself up more times than anybody knows. But this time, accept the hands that seek to support you with this heavy load. *Please, my love, don't do it alone.*

Every part of you isn't for everyone, when your soul is screaming for separation, when their energy starts to consume your air, when they're only concerned about why you're not there yet make no efforts to be there for you. When every conversation leaves you anxious and wondering, "What did I do?" Let these words ring true: *Everybody doesn't deserve access to you.*

Change is inevitable but that doesn't mean it's always fun. It's the thing that we all know is coming but are still always shocked at its arrival, we struggle with the transition of it, at times we don't even notice the transition because it feels too quick, like everything just changed and we struggle with that. We stand at the edge of diving pad, and we swear that if we just jump off, we will drown, we fear that all that we cannot do will somehow weigh us down, but the change pushes us. No matter how many times we tell it we can't, no matter how many times we try to slap it away, change is relentless in its pursuit to see us jump in and just watch everything unfold. It pushes, and pushes and pushes, until we are eventually falling headfirst into the depths of water that swallows us and we panic. We thrash around and wail and scream and beg and plead, and then we stop. We think in that moment that if we stop resisting that we will drown but we float to the surface, we breathe, we sail, as change looks over the end of diving pad and blows us a kiss, for we did not die through change. It was just something that needed to happen to keep us moving beyond our fear.

You deserve a gentle kind of love. The kind of love that makes waking up in the morning a little easier because you know affirming words are awaiting you via text; the kind of love that ensures you eat even when your mind tries to tell you not to; the kind of love that makes you smile aimlessly at nothing in particular; the kind of love that makes you cut off anyone that doesn't love you the way you need to be loved; the kind of love that makes you realise that maybe your self-love needs to be more gentle with affirming words and celebratory dances for the simple things. You deserve a love so gentle that you never accept anything that makes you question whether you deserve to be loved.

I just want you to know that I see you and appreciate you. I see you loving others from such a pure part of your soul. I see the way that you show up for people, even those who do not thank you for such a heartwarming gift. I see you, the person with the heart of gold who refuses to give up on the world that, at times, has made you feel like it gave up on you. I see you in all that you do. I see you loving people through their darkest hours and showering them with the light that you have cultivated from your own journey through such a place. I want you to be receptive to me when I tell you this. I don't want to see you miss out on the best parts of you; you don't deserve to. I love that you love with such vibrancy that it paints the minds of those struggling with hopes brightest hue. People like you are needed in this world, but you cannot pour from emptiness. Please make sure that people are pouring back into you, and you are to, because beautiful soul, *you deserve the best of you.*

I want you to know that you are loved. For all that you are, all that you have been, and all that you will become, you are loved. I have enough space for all of you in my heart and in my life; there is no need to chip at or destroy the facets of the being that brought you here because you think I cannot love it all. Only disrobe yourself of those facets if your soul is calling to grow something new from its absence; do not do it for me. I never want you to see me as the person you sacrificed self for; I want to be the person who welcomed your flaws and made you realise that all of who you are is beautiful and that you are loved. In your entirety, you are loved by me.

I know you don't want to let go. Your mind is still holding onto the warmth of the memories that you both made. You still feel the way that your heart fluttered when you realised how much you had in common. You still remember the way you held each other as you cried freely without feeling weighted by the anxiety of showing your emotions, because with them you found safety. I know you are holding onto all of the good times, but they are asking you to let go. The people you once were cannot return, for you have both evolved beautifully. They are not able to hold on right now, and you too must release them. You cannot make them stay. No matter how much you want to hold onto what was. No matter how much your heart breaks at the idea of life without them. No matter how much you mourn the future you both spoke of. You will only hurt yourself more by running headfirst into a closed door. Maybe it won't be forever. Maybe this ending is just the beginning of something greater. Maybe their job was to show you that you deserve more than you even know. Maybe you were both meant to enter each other's lives and love one another so much that it had to be shared amongst others. But my love, you will never know the lesson to be found in this if you do not allow yourself to let go.

You may not realise it, but your existence is someone's blessing.

I promise you will have good days again. Days where your favourite songs hit your soul as they once did, and your uncoordinated jig will come back as you bare all of your teeth with the wide grin that takes over your face, as the lyrics talk to you and the beat travels through your body. You will be able to eat your favourite foods again, your taste buds will sigh in relief as they did the first time, enjoying the chance to truly experience the journey of flavours. You will be able to respond to calls and messages without bracing yourself for hours beforehand or preparing yourself to voice the responses that they want to hear, because the truth is too much to deal with and too heavy to share with phone to ear. You will fall in love with your dreams again as hope circles you and laughs at the way that your eyes light up as you realise that you have buried something so beautiful and worthy of life. You will smile just because you are here, just because you are special, just because you are worthy, just because you did the very thing you thought you couldn't do; you made it through and returned to you as someone that you truly love. I promise your good days are coming. *Start preparing for your joy.*

The truth is that they won't always get it. Your desire to be loved in such a tender way is why your heart seeks to connect with someone in a beautifully authentic state. They don't realise that it's not because you want someone to love you out of hating yourself, but because you have set yourself in a palace of self-love that cannot be tampered with by someone else, and now you are ready to share yourself. To have someone come into your life and add to the joy that you have cultivated in the years when you were the only person you dated. They don't realise 'it will come when you least expect it' isn't helpful for you to hear because you haven't been expecting it for years, yet your heart still finds itself excited at the prospect of loving and being loved. You are among life's majestically romantic souls; you are Cupid's child, pecked with the love bug, and you celebrate its presence wherever you go. I wonder if they know that all you need is an ear for someone to hear your feelings and fears without making you want to disappear, with the dismissal of your feelings in moments that could be healing if they just tried to understand. There is nothing wrong with you for desiring love. *I hope upon its arrival, it is everything you ever dreamed of.*

It's just a thought, you're okay. I know it feels big and bad and mean and all too real, but it will pass. Sometimes, when I am struggling to breathe beneath the weight of my thoughts, I like to think of them like clouds in the sky. Pieces of candy floss amongst a sea of blue. Constantly moving, even when they feel too close, too big, or too still, I know they will pass me eventually. They cannot help it. That is what they must do. So, I can see the horribly formed clouds that remind me of mean things I have said to myself or have been said to me, or try to show me stories that have never played out but give me anxiety, but I know eventually they will pass and once again a small sense of clarity will return. After some time, I am able to look up and see the other picturesque fluffy miracles that decorate the sky, which remind me of the good to be found and to come. I just have to breathe and let the clouds pass me by.

I know that there is something within you that keeps reciting that you are not loved, but I need you to hear me when I say this. You are loved by me, so fucking loved by me that it honestly hurts sometimes. I didn't know I had the capacity to love with such intensity and intentionality until I met you. I love you from the top of my head to tip of my toe, I love you in your silence, I love you in your tearful laughter that fills up a room and charges us all with a new lease of life, I love you when you cannot text me back because your feelings are too much, I love you when you can sit on the phone with me in silence just sending videos back and forth because just being there with eachother makes our lives feel a little lighter, I love you into tomorrow and all of the days that dare pass us, I love you in the songs that I cannot listen to if I am not listening with you because they just don't bring me the same joy, I love you beyond this period of your life that requires you to put yourself first, and can I just say that I am so proud of you for finally doing it. I understand. Take your time. Just know that my hand is always here, waiting for the returned warmth of yours in mine, so that we can walk aimlessly as if we own the world, because as long as we have each other, we are a beautifully perfect mess. *You Are Loved By Me.*

It is okay to mourn who you once were as you ascend into who you are becoming.

There are days when we just need to cry, and that's okay. I know it's not easy to let yourself feel. Let's cry together. Let's put on that Disney movie that brings us to tears every single time and watch it. Let's enjoy the highs and let our eyes leak until we are just having a full-blown moment and we realise that we are no longer crying about the movie but something entirely different. Let's put on your crying playlist and encourage ourselves to let it all out and feel ourselves crumble into the floor, enjoying its steadiness as we trek through the uncertainty of these feelings that are too wild to tame. Let's catch a glimpse of ourselves in the mirror, and decide whether we are cute or ugly criers, and cry even more at either revelation. Let's just let it all out because we are tired of holding it together. Then, once our weeps have become gentle hiccups and our hearts have placed a heated blanket over our minds, let us snuggle into the warmth of our bed sheets and sleep. A light sleep. An easier to begin sleep. A sleep no longer disrupted by the spillage of feelings we tried to hide. Let's just give ourselves permission to cry.

Sometimes we just need a hug. For someone to hold us so tight that we feel ourselves slot back into place. To soak in the softness of the moment and feel our heart sigh for it has a moment of relief. To sink so deeply into the warmth of another body and give ourselves a moment to breathe. Sometimes we just need to be hugged with such intensity that it places a little bandage upon our unravelling seams.

Oh, my Angel, you might find that you have to cry it out. Let all of those tears leave your body until you are limp and your eyes sting, until you feel your eyes dry heaving because there is nothing left, for your body has purged it all. Cry boldly and let your guttural cries rip through you and roar into the empty ruins of your room, or sob silently if your body calls to. You might have to find your own closure in this by getting through it and not over it, for your mind needs some resolution, but maybe they cannot give it to you right now. You may need to come to terms with letting go of the forever planned, but understand that your heart will still love them, but this time from afar. Love doesn't go at once, it cannot be beckoned and forced into submission. This might take a while, and I know your heart hurts as it breaks, your belly filling up on its shards because you cannot stomach much more.

Oh my love, nothing breaks like the heart

I wish you knew the impact that you have on people's lives. I wish you could see how you have made many weeds bloom into something entirely too beautiful for words to compute, how your smile sets a tone of peace in a hardened room, how your joy settles a blanket upon anxious minds, and how your energy recharges people by simply sitting in your presence. I know that life has dealt you some difficult lessons, but there is something about you that seems to harbour its own perfection, and it seeps into every space that you enter. I wish you knew how much of an impression you have made on the world in such a short stay. I wish you would believe me when I say that there is something so special about you that offers magic to the strain of the everyday.

You are so far from behind. In fact, I would say that you are right on time. Gently aligned with what is yours. You cannot possibly see the beauty that follows you if your focus is on what others have in store; their journey is not yours. You miss every blessing that you ignore. In a year from now, you will realise that life has been happening for you as you bask in the blessings that you prayed for. Trust me, my love, you aren't behind. Be patient; it's all going to happen at the right time.

I thank you for being my light on the days where life feels difficult to love and time seems to trample me because I cannot find peace in its passing. I thank you for smiling when I cannot, for hugging me even when I don't have the energy to hug you back with as much tightness as I would like. I thank you for the love that you show in everything you do, so that I always feel loved. I thank you for being the kind of friend everyone deserves to have. I thank you for being silly and weird with me on my good days and allowing me to love you as you deserve in our friendship. Thank you for letting me be there for you as you are for me, to cherish and be gentle with your heart and mind as we go through life together. I promise you will always have a safe space with me. *I love you*

Your mind has made you believe that nobody cares, but I do! I care so much that my heart hurts to watch you dig into yourself and hide from all who seek to love you. I wish I could trap you in my heart so that you could feel the way it beats in affirming words destined for you to hear. I don't want you to think that you have been forgotten as you go through this journey within yourself. You are searching for fragments of the person you once knew, but I know that there is a fire calling you to lean into the shift of becoming someone new. I will be here waiting to be introduced to whatever version of you emerges from the journey. I need you to know that your name is one of the first in my prayers. I care that you didn't eat today because your body is a treasured palace homing a blessing too precious for this world, your soul. I care about every feeling that crashes through you, each one desiring your full attention, not knowing they are causing a tornado of unbalance within you. I care to sit and hear you speak them through with me, so that they are not harbouring within you and creating narratives that are untrue. I care about all that you do, from brushing your teeth to going to work to struggling to sleep to finally having the energy to eat your favourite treat. I care about you wholly, and my soul aches at the thought that you don't know that my heart is always a home you can find comfort in. *I care for you with all of me.*

Oh, look at you, my little dreamer. With stars in your eyes that shine so brightly as you talk about what is aligned with you, with skin that flushes with an excited hue, with hands that become supporting acts as your mind dances away with you, and you take me on an adventure through your minds wonderland. Oh, my little dreamer, if only you knew what warmth possesses my heart at the sight of you, in the moments of pure joy that consume you as you show me around the landmarks that keep you up at night, that scream for your exploration and call to be created. Oh, beautiful dreamer, such magic is found when you say your dreams out loud. I can't wait to see them come true, for they *can only be done by you.*

I don't think you are too much; I think you are perfectly enough, bountiful in the way you shine in a world that fizzles the rawness of our light. With time, we stop realising how privileged we are to shine with a fire that was only destined for us. This world is filled with people who wish that they were courageous enough to be their fullest selves, and then there is you, a soul so comfortable with self that you cannot help but glow shamelessly in a world that fears the boundless nature of fearless souls. I ask that you allow yourself to be too much; glow, spin, sing, and prance until you are flushed and filled with fits of giggles. Show us all that it is safe and beautiful to be too much for others but perfectly enough for yourself.

My love, the mind of the dreamer is not one that is meant to be understood by just anyone. It is a playground filled with destinations that are perfectly designed with you in mind, so intricately personalised that only you can see the rawest form of the magic that can derive from such beautifully bundled chaos. To some, this wonderland will feel too big and out of touch, but that's the beauty of the dreamers. They make too much, into perfectly enough and something to share. Dreamers, do not do not fear the dreams and thoughts that you hear, trust yourself and watch your wonderland appear.

It is coming. I know you are scared and filled with uncertainty. I know that every step forward feels like a careful tread because you have fears of fully committing and trusting that it will all work out this time. It will. You might not see it, but there is such beauty calling your name and begging you to keep moving forward. Begging you to trust yourself, begging you to listen to that little tickle at the back of your mind that keeps on reminding you that it is your time, and you are aligned. I need you to keep moving forward because your blessings are running towards you. *Trust Yourself*

If only they knew what you go through. If they heard the secrets that your walls hold in hopes that one day you will open the door and let them sing your sorrows into the ears of someone who can help, You smile amongst groups of people with a shine that very few can put their finger on, but I see it, the glow that comes from wanting to put out into the world what you have not received. I know it personally. You want to save people, yet you refuse to save yourself. But the truth is, you need yourself more. I can't tell you what to do, but I hope you make time dedicated to only you. Whether that is finding someone to talk to or learning to be a friend to yourself, you can't keep going as you're going. It's not good for your health. Please Hear Me *My Love, You Need You More.*

Oh, my love, they use selfish as if it is inherently bad, but when do they decide to call you that? When you set boundaries, when you tell them you haven't got time, when you tell them you need a second to take care of your mind, what beautifully selfish acts you are doing, and I think you should do them more. It's not selfish to take care of the peace that you had to fight for.

One day I hope that you are restored with compassion for yourself. I watch you pull yourself apart in hopes that you will find all of your faults. I have yet to see you do something so cruel to anyone that surrounds you. I see you speak acceptance and love over them. I see you showing them that it is okay that they are not feeling like their best selves right now. I see you reminding them that they are perfect, even if they don't always feel like that, because who they are right now, is perfectly who they need to be for this period of their lives. I see you wipe their tears and hold them gently and lovingly. I wonder sometimes how beautifully you would thrive if you gave yourself a little of that compassion. *My Love, You Are Worthy Of Your Gentleness.*

We have a tendency to forget to give ourselves the things that we needed but weren't given by people in our lives. And if there is one thing I ask that you do, it's that you cultivate the kind of life that makes the outside noise a gentle hum amongst the beauty of the jazz that flows through your life. You have always deserved the best.

I just want you to know that you are doing a great job. I know there are things that you are battling in silence and nobody around you truly realises how hard you are working to show up for yourself and them. I see you; I want you to know that I am proud of you for getting out of bed, brushing your teeth, showering, and nourishing your body. I know the basics can feel so difficult when you're in a space where your mind is drowning, and you are still having to figure out how to live life at the same time, trying not to give in to the mind's desire to no longer try. I know even when you're smiling you have a war happening inside, I'm sorry you're dealing with so much. I want you to know I dream of seeing you truly smile, of days where your heart feels lighter, and the promise of the future leaves a brighter hue surrounding you. I just wanted you to know, *I am always thinking of you.*

There will be moments when you just can't. Can't sleep, can't stay awake, can't eat, can't get out of bed, feel like you can't get through the day. But then you get that little glimpse of can. Sometimes it's finally being able to get up to brush your teeth after 3 days, but it reminds you that you can, and with time, things can get better and easier.

If I could pour peace on anyone, it would be you. I find the cards that you have been dealt to be too cruel for the loving nature that you exude. Where becoming hardened and desensitised seems a more fitting survival tool, I watch you dance with your emotions; at times, I watch them trample you. But you seem to smile through it all, and people seem to enjoy the dance and avoid each other's glances in the moments when you tumble. I wish that I could take hold of you and offer you a space to sit with your emotions, to not feel like you have to constantly keep them entertained. Even in your lightness, my love, you are still heavy, decorated with wounds that were never yours to tend to, and yet you do. You find excuses for all that causes you pain in the name of being humane, and I wish nothing more than to give you my apologies for the burden you carry. It is not yours, but I realise that you would rather hold it. Rather, be the one to keep a tight leash on such a thing so that you do not do to others as has been done to you. I wish you didn't live that way; I wish I could pour peace onto you and watch your wounds fade away. *My Love, You Deserve Peace.*

You might not see it, but I think that you are among some of the most beautiful beings to bless this Earth. You are a gentle soul living in a world of madness, and, my love, I know it takes much strength. To love and care with such intensity that other's misfortunes bring you to tears; to be filled with so much joy that their success fulfils you as if it were your own; to want to save people and sit with the realisation that you can't save everybody. What a gift it is to be in touch with your rawest self! What a magical thing it is to allow yourself to be vulnerable and let us see you for who you really are. And I thank you for such a gift. I thank you for showing up in life with your silent strength and comforting glow. Thank you for being "too sensitive."

Oh, my love, life can be beautiful. It can, it can, it can. I am realising that it's not the big moments. God, no. It's in the small moments, the seemingly insignificant moments, that we take for granted and often miss because we are waiting for the big thing. It's the smile that sneaks onto your face at the picture of a cat, the way mother nature sneaks the sun through your blinds and casts golden patterns that dance all over your room, the brief but beautiful interaction between you and a stranger as you collect your coffee, the childish glee of watching a childhood cartoon, the little happy dance you do when you eat your favourite food, or the sigh of relief when you get back into your warm bed sheets. Gosh, I have found such beauty in life by finding gratitude for these small moments. It's not easy, I know, to see the little pockets of beauty surrounding you when you are surrounded by pain, but I promise you, one day you will see them decorated all over your life, and you will realise all of the little blessings that follow you.

Make time for the people who make you feel safe in the face of days that are hard to stomach.

Fall into my heart and let it bathe you of the wounds that were never yours to bear. Let my love speak truths into the corners of your mind that you hide from. Let my arms keep you up when you feel too weak to do life. Let my eyes see the you that you try to disguise. Let me remind your inner child that they are deserving of life and give them comfort in knowing that I am not someone who will leave your side. I am in this with you. Through the tears, the silence, the bathless days, and the moments where your mind leaves me alone in our space, I am here for you. I promise we will see this through. I can't save you, but I can show you what I mean when I say,

I love you.

You deserve to live, I don't know what those wicked voice try to convince you that you are, but my love your heart soothes the soreness of the world, your laugh is a symphony of hope in a room of the heavy hearted, your smile is a promise of new day to those that fear that life could never change, your eyes show that whilst we may go through pain, there is hope for a better tomorrow to come our way, your hugs allow people to exhale for the first time as they unwind and allow their souls a moment to just rest and reconnect to the warmth of a soul like your own that has always sought to see people happy, your voice is filled with promise that every day is a chance to move forward because despite all that you have encountered, you have not lost your voice. I promise you, my love, those voices lie, and if you ever have to ask yourself why you should fight, remember that I know that you are deserving of peace-filled life.

Sensitive souls see the way that the world explodes with colours even on the gloomiest days when the clouds gang up on the sun and bully it to the back of the room. They see her calls in the shop window or the tingle at the back of their neck, and it is a wonderful prospect to know that we share the world with those gifted with the power of sensitivity. Those whose eyes fill with tears at the idea of a pain that they have never felt, but understand because of the way that their stomach burns with a desire to take all pain from you, the wrong people don't know what to do with these angels, for they do not understand what it is like feeling everything with a fullness that doesn't make space for deep breaths to soothe exhaustion of breath taken. These souls need a gentle hand, someone to understand that they feel the good as much as the bad, but the bad is burdened with a weight that shoves head into pillows and burps unshed tears to release. The seemingly 'too sensitive' souls are too precious for a world that wants us all to stop feeling, but we need them all; they are the reason we can find the joy of dancing in the sky's tears, laugh at ice cream moustaches on days that leave us empty and sunken, and cry at movies that bring us such an overwhelming sense of happiness that we feel like our hearts may combust if we don't let our tears out. The too sensitive are perfectly sensitive, indeed.

You cannot pick your flowers from the root before they bloom and then wonder why your soil cannot trust the new life that you try to plant each month.

Your heart is not to be made into a home; you are allowing people to build upon sacred ground, only to leave when they get the gold that they find in the holiness of a heart that beats with the purity of God's softest souls. The body knows, you mistook wasps for butterflies because the winded feeling was enough of a rush for clarity to be thrown away. You welcomed them and watched them chip little pieces of your peace to make space for their own. You watched them build home as you remained homeless within your own heart because you hadn't been encouraged to be a receiver of the healing that was harboured within your heart's grounds. It breaks my heart to watch you sit beneath windowpanes and look into the homes, both new and abandoned, as you remain in your sleeping bag, waiting for someone to offer you an inn. Oh, my love, your heart is not to be made a home, especially if it is not a home of your own.

It may fall apart before it falls in line.

Your heart is breaking, a little, too much, too often; specs of your hope are drowned in the shower as the water swallows your yells, and your body wants nothing more than to curl into itself. You are being forced to face all that you are not, and it is a brutal awakening to see everything fall apart and not piece itself together into a wonder of art. The pieces are itching for you to face them, to lay them upon your head, to put on your favourite song, and to find the calling in their perishing. In all that you are not, you are faced with all that you are.

I am here, even if I am not near, and my voice is hard to hear beneath the chaos of the thoughts that fight for your attention. If you look down at your phone, I have named myself home, so that you know you can always come back to me. There is no place that your mind could take you that would be too far for me to come and pick you up from; my love for you runs beyond the pain of your present and the fruits of your future. I am here, loving you through it all.

If they knew, I like to think that they would have done better by you. I'm sorry.

@m.musecreates